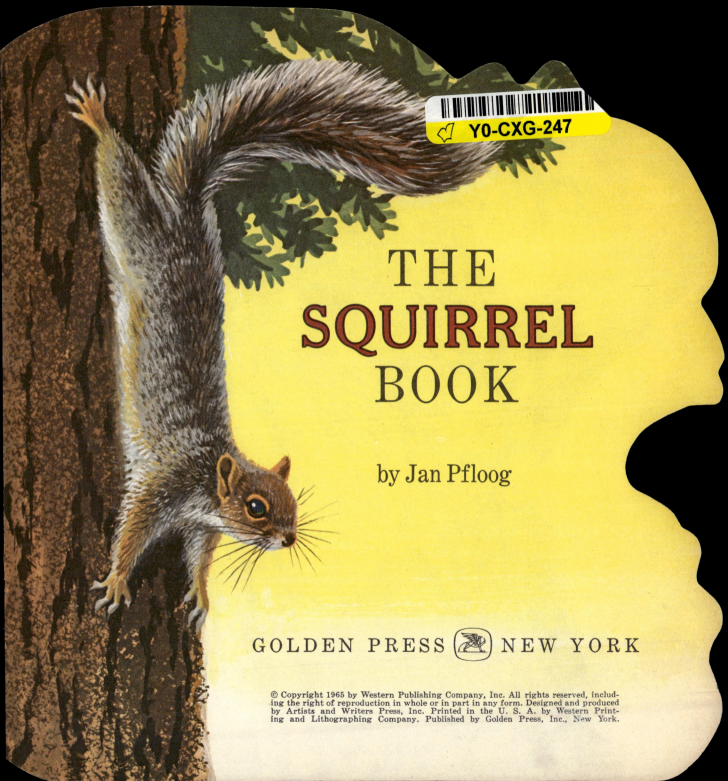

THE
SQUIRREL
BOOK

by Jan Pfloog

GOLDEN PRESS 🦅 NEW YORK

This is a Gray Squirrel.
He lives in a tree.

Gray Squirrel
eats all kinds
of seeds and nuts.

This is his summer nest.
Blue jay is paying him a visit.

In the fall Gray Squirrel buries
nuts to save them for winter.

When the snow comes and food is hard to find he digs up the nuts...

and eats them
in his warm
winter nest.

Mother Gray Squirrel
is teaching her babies
how to jump from tree to tree.

These Gray Squirrels
live in a city park.

They are very friendly.

A Fox Squirrel is the biggest
kind of squirrel.

This is a Southern Fox Squirrel.
He is saying hello to his friend
the Chipmunk.

Red Squirrel is small and noisy and nosy.
He scolds EVERYONE that walks by.

This is a Tassel-Eared Squirrel. He wears the fanciest coat of all the squirrels and lives near the Grand Canyon.

Chickaree lives in the west. He is always chittering and chattering noisily.

The Flying Squirrel comes out at night.
He doesn't really fly, but glides long
distances from one tree to another.
He is the smallest of the tree squirrels.